SHARPENING YOUR TONGUE

A REGNUM CHRISTI ESSAY ON CHARITY IN OUR WORDS

FR. JOHN BARTUNEK, LC, STHD

ISBN-10: 0692633510

ISBN-13: 978-0692633519

RC Essay Editorial Review Board:

Fr. John Bartunek, LC, SThD
Fr. Daniel Brandenburg, LC, PhL, SThL
Lucy Honner, CRC
Rebecca Teti, *CatholicDigest.com* writer and editor

TABLE OF CONTENTS

FOREWORD

FOREWORD: WHAT ARE RC ESSAYS?

RC Essays are extended, in-depth reflections on particular aspects of life as a Regnum Christi member. An Essay may develop the nature of a virtue, showing what that virtue might look like when lived out in harmony with the Regnum Christi identity and mission. An Essay may explore the challenges of living out one of the commitments shared by all members. An Essay may be instructive, explaining the history, context, and meaning of certain Movement traditions. In short, RC Essays are a chance for all of us to delve deeper into our charism, reflecting seriously on our spiritual patrimony, which the Church has recognized and lauded, and in that way helping that patrimony grow and bear fruit.

RC Essays make no pretense of being the sole and exhaustive expression of our charism. The RC Spirituality Center will review and edit them to ensure their quality in expression and content, but no single person owns a collective charism in such a way as to give it a definitive and exhaustive expression. This is one of the important lessons we have begun to learn in our process of reform and renewal.

Some RC Essays will lend themselves naturally to personal meditation; others will be especially apt for group study circles; all aim to be useful as spiritual reading for members in every branch of the Movement.

It is our hope and prayer that this series will continue to grow organically under the Holy Spirit's guidance. Some Essays will connect more strongly with our members, and others less, while some may fall by the wayside after their useful moment has passed. Yet perhaps the best RC Essays will stand the test of time, becoming spiritual and intellectual nourishment for many generations of Movement members.

Please send your ideas and feedback to us through the feedback button at RCSpirituality.org.

SHARPENING YOUR TONGUE

INTRODUCTION

In the Regnum Christi Movement, we have always emphasized the importance of charity in words. Not that we invented the concept—on the contrary, the power of words to work good or ill is an unmistakable biblical motif. Yet in Regnum Christi we have always given special attention to this arena of Christian virtues.

Unfortunately, as long-term members of the Movement can attest to, our understanding of exactly what charity in words looks like has sometimes been skewed. For a long time the Movement's culture focused so much on the concept of "well-speaking" (*benediciencia* in Spanish) that we tended to neglect developing the skills and virtues necessary for engaging in healthy conflict and constructive criticism. It was often (and wrongly) thought that any comment with a whiff of negativity (whatever that might mean) would automatically qualify as a fault against charity. Fraternal correction suffered because of this. Substantial and useful feedback was sometimes suffocated: member-to-member, member-to-director, and member-to-Movement.

This distortion likely flowed, at least in part, from the overly centralized authority structure of the Movement, as well as from an immature understanding of the relationship between the founder of an ecclesial movement and the charism God gives to that movement. And in our case those factors were surely exacerbated by how the founder's double life impacted our internal communication culture.

Nevertheless the emphasis we have put on using words to build each other up instead of break each other down also has had positive repercussions. I still remember how freeing and refreshing it was to experience for the first time the atmosphere of mutual acceptance in Legionary houses of formation. We simply *knew* that no one was talking about us behind our back. We just didn't have to worry about that kind of thing. Never before had I been part of a community where that was the case.

How can we keep the good and correct the bad? A calm, systematic reflection on what charity in words truly consists of may help. That is the goal of this RC Essay. We will start by reviewing the different types of sin the Church has always warned us against regarding our use of words. Then we will explore the vast horizon of virtue in this field, trying to see what spiritual maturity looks like there, and how to grow in that maturity.

WORDS MATTER

Among God's visible creations, language belongs exclusively to human beings. Other species communicate, and some can even learn to communicate in a limited fashion with us, but language itself eludes them. This is why not even specially trained animals spontaneously start composing songs or writing poetry. This is why scientists have never found hidden, underwater libraries frequented by dolphin pods. This is why, although a dog may reside with a family for its entire lifetime, it never develops an ability to speak even as rudimentarily as a three-year-old child. The capacity for abstract thinking and reasoning (the lifeblood of language) is a spiritual capacity, and of all God's visible creations, only human beings have a spiritual soul.

Our ability to communicate through language—to sit around the living room and have a conversation filled with passion, laughter, tears, and mutual discoveries, for example— somehow likens us to God. It's connected to being created in his image and likeness: "In the beginning was the Word, and the Word was with God, and the Word was God" (John 1:1). God is pure spirit, and the Blessed Trinity mysteriously participates in mutual knowledge and communication, spiritual realities accessible through language. From this perspective it is no coincidence that Adam's first job had to do with language:

> So the Lord God formed out of the ground all the wild animals and all the birds of the air, and he brought them to the man to see *what he would call them*; whatever the man called each living creature was then its name. *The man gave names* to all the tame animals, all the birds of the air, and all the wild animals...
>
> ——Genesis 2:19–20, emphasis added

Naming things, knowing things, communicating our knowledge to others and receiving their communications—these activities touch the core of who we are as human beings. They propel us forward and make us grow, as individuals and as cultures: "Truth in words, the rational expression of the knowledge of created and uncreated reality, is necessary to man, who is endowed with intellect" (*CCC*, 2500) Without language, without words, we would be stuck forever within the limitations of mere instinct, no better than the wild beasts. Our capacity for language matters. It matters a lot.

When the devil sallied forth to disrupt God's plan for the human family, he laid his trap by abusing language—by means of a calculated lie. Indeed, the capacity for language finds its moral anchor in truth, because "men could not live with one another if there were not a mutual confidence that they were being truthful to one another," as St. Thomas Aquinas put it. The Book of Genesis describes the devil's conversation with Eve as the first violation of truth, full of subtle deception and seductive flattery. And Jesus himself calls the devil a "liar and the father of lies" (John 8:44). Original sin itself, then, was triggered by an abuse of this spiritual capacity for language. Evil words well spoken shattered our first parents' trust in God's goodness, opening the door to disobedience and inundating the world with sin (see *CCC*, 397–401).

3

And how does God take away that sin? How is Christ's redeeming sacrifice on Calvary applied to our sins, freeing us from their bondage? Christ, the *Word* (see John 1:1ff) himself, does this through the *words* of all the sacraments, none of which can be celebrated without its specific verbal "form" (e.g., the words "I baptize you in the name of the Father, and of the Son, and of the Holy Spirit..."), which gives meaning and saving power to its specific "matter" (e.g., the *water* in baptism). Most directly, when we repent of our personal sins, we are cleansed from them by the *words* of absolution: "I absolve you from your sins..." The whole sacramental economy involves God's Word of mercy reversing the devil's word of destruction. Through the words of the tempter came the fall of creation, but through words of grace comes forth a new heaven and earth, the redeemed kingdom of Christ that will last forever.

A BIBLICAL PERSPECTIVE

Words matter so much that using them well constitutes one of the main motifs of moral behavior throughout the entire Bible. We will come back to some of these passages later in this Essay, but mentioning them right at the outset will help put us on solid ground.

Jesus linked what we say with our mouths to what we truly have in our hearts, showing that the quality of our words is directly connected with the moral and spiritual state of our souls. He made this comment when discussing with the Pharisees the relative unimportance of merely external rituals (such as dietary restrictions) in the pursuit of holiness.

Hypocrites, well did Isaiah prophesy about you when he said: 'This people honors me with their lips, but their hearts are far from me; in vain do they worship me, teaching as doctrines human precepts.' He summoned the crowd and said to them, 'Hear and understand. It is not what enters one's mouth that defiles that person; but what comes out of the mouth is what defiles one.'

—Matthew 15:7–11, 12:34

In another exchange with his critics, he put it even more succinctly: "You brood of vipers, how can you say good things when you are evil? For from the fullness of the heart the mouth speaks" (Matthew 12:34).

Notice how Jesus begins his instruction on this point with a quotation from the Old Testament, where the power of words and the importance of honesty and prudence in speech appear frequently, most especially in the wisdom literature. Proverbs 18:21 gives what may be the most concise summary of this power: "Death and life are in the power of the tongue; those who choose one shall eat its fruit."

The Book of Psalms often uses imagery of weapons when describing the damage worked by evil words.

I must lie down in the midst of lions
hungry for human prey.
Their teeth are spears and arrows;
their tongue, a sharpened sword.

—Psalm 57:5

Hide me from the malicious crowd,
the mob of evildoers.
They sharpen their tongues like swords,
bend their bows of poison words.

—Psalm 64:3–4

Deliver me, LORD, from the wicked;
preserve me from the violent,

> From those who plan evil in their hearts,
> who stir up conflicts every day,
> Who sharpen their tongue like a serpent,
> venom of asps upon their lips.

—Psalm 140:2–4

In all three examples, the evil enemies commit their crimes not only through actions, but also through words. Evil words cause deadly damage.

In his New Testament Letter, St. James picks up on this same theme. He not only shows the apparently disproportionate impact of such a small organ as the tongue, but he also explicitly links virtue in speech with spiritual maturity. He writes:

> Not many of you should become teachers, my brothers, for you realize that we will be judged more strictly, for we all fall short in many respects.
>
> If anyone does not fall short in speech, he is a perfect man, able to bridle his whole body also. If we put bits into the mouths of horses to make them obey us, we also guide their whole bodies. It is the same with ships: even though they are so large and driven by fierce winds, they are steered by a very small rudder wherever the pilot's inclination wishes. In the same way the tongue is a small member and yet has great pretensions. Consider how small a fire can set a huge forest ablaze.
>
> The tongue is also a fire. It exists among our members as a world of malice, defiling the whole body and setting the entire course of our lives on fire, itself set on fire by Gehenna. For every kind of beast and bird, of reptile and sea creature, can be tamed and has been tamed by the human species, but no human being can tame the tongue. It is a restless evil, full of deadly poison. With

it we bless the Lord and Father, and with it we curse human beings who are made in the likeness of God. From the same mouth come blessing and cursing. This need not be so, my brothers.

—James 3:1–10

Evil or foolish words cause damage—sometimes horrible damage. These biblical passages make that clear. Yet the Bible's descriptions tell us only what we have all experienced: the blow that comes from being slandered or wickedly criticized takes a long time—sometimes a lifetime—to lose its sting.

Evil words only work such great mischief, however, because the power of words has such great potential for good. "The corruption of the best is the worst," as Aristotle put it. Yes, evil men "sharpen their tongues like swords," but a sharp sword can be useful for good as well as for evil. A sharp knife is necessary for proper surgery and good cooking; a sharp axe is more effective for chopping wood than a dull one. Words can be used to sin, but as St. James points out, "This need not be so." Mature virtue in speech requires a sharp tongue—a tongue well trained in the use of words—just as much as horribly vicious speech does.

So much good can be done with our words! The more we understand and master virtue and skill in this arena, the more good we can do with everything we say.

St. Paul expresses this multiple times in his New Testament writings. He almost always refers to virtuous speech—speech that builds up the community and spreads goodness—in his lists of essentially Christian behaviors. In his Letter to the Colossians, for example, he writes: "Let your speech always be gracious, seasoned with salt, so that you know how you should respond to each one" (Colossians 4:6). His Letter to the Ephesians goes into more detail:

> Therefore, putting away falsehood, speak the truth, each one to his neighbor, for we are members one of another.... No foul language should come out of your mouths, but only such as is good for needed edification, that it may impart grace to those who hear.

> —Ephesians 4:25, 29

Words really do matter. Our words can "impart grace," according to St. Paul, edifying (building up) Christ's kingdom in our hearts and the hearts of our neighbors. Our words, in short, can be vehicles of salvation, just as they can be vehicles of destruction: "Death and life are in the power of the tongue" (Proverbs 18:21). Sharpening our tongue for good involves learning which forms of evil and carelessness in speech we need to avoid and which forms of virtue we need to develop. We will turn to those topics now.

WHAT'S IN A LIE?

Sins in speech, and in all forms of communication, are abuses of this spiritual capacity for language. The proper use of language always builds up the human community by communicating truth. Its abuse, on the other hand, wounds and destroys by somehow violating the truth, though it may hold out some temporary benefit to the abuser.

The *Catechism* lists essential sins in this area when it discusses the Eighth Commandment: "Thou shalt not bear false witness against your neighbor." Lying constitutes the most direct abuse of our ability to communicate through language. The *Catechism* defines lying in this way: "to speak or act against the truth in order to lead someone into error" (*CCC*, 2483). Lying, as we all know from experience, almost always breeds more lying. When we start covering up the truth, we then have to start covering up our cover-ups, and the fragile scaffolding of falsehoods continues to grow until it collapses in a heap of ignominy, hurt, and just plain embarrassment.

But what about so-called white lies? When someone bakes you a cake and asks how it is, are you required to say "Dry as a bone!" if that is how it tastes to you? Is it a sin against the truth to simply say, "Delicious!" in order to spare the person's feelings?

And what about lying in order to protect the innocent? Catholics in seventeenth-century England colluded in disguising and hiding priests, whom the laws of the land considered traitors. Priests in England during those times intentionally deceived their enemies into thinking that they weren't priests, so as to be able to continue their ministry in secret. Were these deceptions sinful?

Even learned and honest theologians can get tangled up trying to sort through thorny cases like these. This is because morality is not mathematics. Certainly right and wrong exist in morality, just as they exist in mathematics. But what is clearly right and wrong at the level of principle ("Thou shalt not bear false witness against thy neighbor") can become muddy and confusing five or six levels removed, when principles have to be applied amidst the complexities of everyday life in this fallen world.

We cannot pretend to resolve every possible dilemma with some kind of magic moral formula. And yet most of us would instinctually feel that what those Catholics did under persecution in England was morally upright. And a white lie that does no harm to anyone and avoids causing unnecessary emotional distress seems to be acceptable as well, on some level. Our Catholic wisdom, accumulated through the centuries, provides several principles to help us understand those instincts.

The *Catechism* points out, for example, that "the right to the communication of truth is not unconditional" (*CCC*, 2488). Truth is at the service of justice and charity, of fair and fruitful relations between people. In some circumstances, then, prudence may indicate that justice and charity are better served by silence or secrets than by a full explanation or exposure of everything involved.

Everyone must conform his life to the Gospel precept of fraternal love. This requires us in concrete situations to judge whether or not it is appropriate to reveal the truth to someone who asks for it. Charity and respect for the truth should dictate the response to every *request for information or communication.* The good and safety of others, respect for privacy, and the common good are sufficient reasons for being silent about what ought not be known or for making use of a discreet language. The duty to avoid scandal often commands strict discretion. No one is bound to reveal the truth to someone who does not have the right to know it.

—*CCC,* 2488–2489

The point here is not to give us an excuse for whimsically playing fast and loose with the truth. Rather we are simply recognizing that words really do have an effect on people's lives, and so we want to be careful with them. We have no right to go around deceiving people in order to build up personal kingdoms of wealth and popularity. But neither should we indiscriminately expose everything we know about everyone to everyone else, regardless of context and heedless of consequences. "Truthfulness keeps to the just mean between what ought to be expressed and what ought to be kept secret: it entails honesty and discretion" (*CCC,* 2469).

We know this instinctually and do it all the time. The conversations you have with your best friend differ considerably from the conversations you have with your bank teller or postal worker. The relationship is different, and so the amount and depth of communication is different. When strangers or mere acquaintances begin to pry into aspects of your life that have nothing to do with them, you are perfectly justified in saying, "I am sorry, but that is none of your business."

At times, however, it is hard to know how much to say or how to be appropriately discreet in saying it. But those are the *extraordinary* situations. For them, the best rule of thumb—the closest thing to a magic moral formula—is simply the Golden Rule of doing to others whatever we would have them to do us. "The golden rule helps one discern, in concrete situations, whether or not it would be appropriate to reveal the truth to someone who asks for it" (*CCC*, 2510).

Well-formed Christians sometimes become obsessed with analyzing these extraordinary situations. They long to eliminate all gray areas in this regard. Yet that will never happen. The specific, concrete situations in which only prudence can judge how much of the truth is too much for the particular circumstance, or how to wield discretion for the preservation of trust, honor, and charity are inexhaustible. We cannot fit them all into formulae. Obsessing over them in the abstract can be a distraction, and one with unpleasant consequences. We need to accept that, although the principles are clear and firm, their application will not always be easy, especially on those rare, extraordinary occasions when we feel that the slightest wrong word could yield disaster.

THE NORMAL TEMPTATIONS

Our ordinary interactions, on the other hand, are rarely plagued by legitimately confounding moral dilemmas. Instead they are beset by simple temptations to fudge the truth or manipulate it in order to placate our vanity, pride, or laziness. We must habitually recognize and resist these temptations in order to develop the virtue of truthfulness, which St. James equates with moral perfection: "If anyone does not fall short in speech, he is a perfect man, able to bridle his whole body also" (James 3:2).

The most common sins against truthfulness in speech and communication—besides outright lying—are listed in the *Catechism* and include rash judgment, calumny, flattery, and boasting. Other sins abusing the power of language adhere to the truth, but use the truth as a weapon of unjust attack instead of an instrument promoting justice and charity. These include detraction, disparaging irony, and destructive criticism. We will touch briefly on each one of these faults in order to clear the way for an ample treatment of virtue in communication.

RASH JUDGMENT

Rash judgment sometimes remains at the level of thought only: interior words spoken by oneself to oneself. But more often than not, rash judgment also eventually makes its way into speech or writing. Jesus himself pointed this out: "But the things that come out of the mouth come from the heart" (Matthew 15:18). It makes sense, then, to begin our reflection on faults in speech with a reflection on one of their deepest roots.

A rash judgment consists of "assuming as true, without sufficient foundation, the moral fault of a neighbor" (*CCC*, 2477). Our fallen nature makes us quick to condemn others. We have a built-in tendency to jump from observable facts ("She seems overdressed for this luncheon") to unobservable motives ("She is so vain"). Doing this somehow feeds our own vanity and pride, which have such voracious appetites. Elevating ourselves to the judgment seat feels good; it gives us an air of superiority.

And yet the truth is that we actually cannot see all the motivations behind why people do what they do. Even when we see someone perform an action that is objectively wrong (a thief stealing a car, for example), we are not privy to the vast interior web of conscious and subconscious motivations behind that action. The action is sinful, without a doubt, and we should feel no need to excuse it. But the path that led this particular person to this particular point in his life may reduce (or increase) significantly his culpability in committing that sin. As soon as we assume that we can see clearly enough to evaluate accurately that culpability—and let ourselves do so—we are falling into rash judgment. This temptation has a pithy old saying for its antidote: "Judge the sin, not the sinner."

Jesus made shockingly stark comments about this behavior. He left no room for doubt about its maliciousness:

> Stop judging, that you may not be judged. For as you judge, so will you be judged, and the measure with which you measure will be measured out to you. Why do you notice the splinter in your brother's eye, but do not perceive the wooden beam in your own eye? How can you say to your brother, 'Let me remove that splinter from your eye,' while the wooden beam is in your eye? You hypocrite, remove the wooden beam from your eye first; then you will see clearly to remove the splinter from your brother's eye.

—Matthew 7:1–5

Sometimes we make the mistake of interpreting this passage as a command against seeing reality the way it is ("I caught him in a lie, but I am not supposed to judge him, so I will pretend that he didn't lie"). Yet that is absurd. Some actions are wrong, whether sinful or mistaken or imprudent. When we perceive that, we are simply acknowledging reality. To twist ourselves into knots in order to convince ourselves that what we have perceived is actually not what we have perceived is the road to insanity. That cannot be what Jesus was talking about.

Rather, the Lord is exhorting us to keep the circle of judgment open, to let God alone be the judge of the whole interior world of hidden motivations and moral culpability. In other words we are called to have a default setting that gives other people the benefit of the doubt on the level of moral culpability. To quote the *Catechism* again: "To avoid rash judgment, everyone should be careful to interpret insofar as possible his neighbor's thoughts, words, and deeds in a favorable way" (*CCC*, 2478).

When we don't do this, Jesus pointed out, we fall into hypocrisy. In our own case, we apply the benefit of the doubt all the time. We automatically give ourselves excuses. If we pull out of the driveway too quickly, cutting someone off, we are sorry about it, but we give ourselves a break— we just didn't see the other car coming. Yet when we are in the other car and someone cuts us off, our initial reaction is usually anger and condemnation (and maybe an obnoxious and unnecessary honk of the horn). We don't give the other person the break we would give ourselves. But we should. That's how we love our neighbors as ourselves. That's how we exercise mercy—not ignoring the evil that is committed, but refraining from issuing a definitive moral judgment against the one who commits that evil. We simply don't have enough information to do that. Only God does.

Thomas à Kempis, in his classic work, *The Imitation of Christ*, comments on this tendency:

You are well versed in coloring your own actions with excuses which you will not accept from others, though it would be more just to accuse yourself and excuse your brother. If you wish men to bear with you, you must bear with them.

He includes this observation in a chapter entitled "Goodness and Peace in Man." Neither goodness nor peace can be had without truth. And rash judgment compromises the truth because it claims more knowledge than it is possible for us humans to have; it pretends to see the whole interior story behind an exterior action, something only God can do.

In another passage, Thomas à Kempis puts into his own words what Jesus said about removing our own splinters before attempting to remove our neighbors' wooden beams:

Try to bear patiently with the defects and infirmities of others, whatever they may be, because you also have many a fault which others must endure.

Rash judgment is an offspring of pride, of the inordinate attachment to self that refuses to admit and accept one's own limitations and remain content to let God be God.

CALUMNY AND SLANDER

Another fault against truth in communication is calumny, which impels other people to end up making false judgments. Here is the *Catechism*'s definition of calumny:

He becomes guilty of calumny who, by remarks contrary to the truth, harms the reputation of others and gives occasion for false judgments concerning them.

—*CCC*, 2477

Simply put, calumny consists of telling lies about other people. It is also known as slander. Sometimes these lies reach egregious proportions ("He's having an affair!"), but often they are so subtle—taking the form of small exaggerations, for example—that they fit right into our daily discourse ("My wife never does the dishes; our kitchen sink is always full of them, and I am the only one who seems to care!"). Another example is sharing on a social media platform a meme or comment that calumniates an entire business or simply assumes bad faith regarding a politician).

Calumnies create havoc. They tarnish a person's good name, and occasionally the damage lasts a lifetime. We should avoid them like the plague. And yet we don't. Here again we encounter temptations that are hard to resist. A little lie here about a competitor can give my bid for a project a bit of an edge. Another lie over there can swing someone's loyalty over to my side, giving me more practical leverage and a psychological sense of affirmation. Calumny can be used as a weapon of revenge, ambition, popularity, or greed. It's a handy tool, if what we're after is a quick and selfish victory regardless of the consequences. But erecting careers, reputations, relationships, or personal kingdoms on a foundation filled with victims of calumny is even worse than building on sand. Both are unstable, but at least sand doesn't reek with the corpselike smell of moral degradation.

FLATTERY AND ADULATION

As strange as it may seem, flattery is akin to calumny. Flattery and adulation, like calumny, depart from the truth. Instead of intending to harm someone, however, these faults seek to win someone's approval or affirmation. Flattery is excessive and insincere praise. Flattering someone requires saying something we believe is untrue, even if it is only a subtle exaggeration. Adulation takes flattery one step further. It is a kind of self-imposed blindness by which we simply refuse to recognize another person's limitations; we convince ourselves that he or she can do no wrong, and we defend even his or her shortcomings against objective criticism.

Both of these faults find their roots in our own insecurities, because both of them seek to obtain affirmation from others through praising them. Instead of showing an unqualified commitment to the truth, flattery and adulation express a neediness on our part, a sometimes barely conscious and sometimes desperate groping for approval and validation. They spring from our tendency toward vanity. Less often, they can also be forms of prideful manipulation. We use flattery in order to win people's trust so we can ride on their coattails and get something from them, or get them to do something for us. When we obtain what we were after, we leave them behind, showing that our appreciation for them was feigned. Here is how the *Catechism* refers to these faults against the truth:

Every word or attitude is forbidden which by flattery, adulation, or complaisance encourages and confirms another in malicious acts and perverse conduct. Adulation is a grave fault if it makes one an accomplice in another's vices or grave sins. Neither the desire to be of service nor friendship justifies duplicitous speech. Adulation is a venial sin when it only seeks to be agreeable, to avoid evil, to meet a need, or to obtain legitimate advantages.

———*CCC*, 2480

These abuses appear to be extreme. When we are striving to live in God's grace, our conscience usually keeps us safe from such wild perversions. But flattery can also tempt us in more subtle ways. As Regnum Christi members, we make a commitment to live Christian charity intentionally, and this involves developing the capacity of *benediciencia*, or "well-speaking." This consists of speaking well about people when they are not around, as opposed to constantly pointing out their faults. It also includes speaking well about people when we are engaged in conversation with them by being encouraging and affirming. But this can go too far. In our efforts to speak well of people, efforts that may be motivated by sincere respect and love, we can end up distorting the truth.

We see this, for example, when we praise someone's external behavior as if it were automatically a result of moral virtue. For instance, in the Legionary novitiate we stress the importance of learning to live exterior silence as a means to foster interior recollection—an important quality for a deepening life of prayer. In my own experience, I remember how some of the novices were really good at external silence, while others were not. There was always a tendency to praise Brother Bo because he never broke silence: "Brother Bo has an incredible interior life—he never talks in the dormitories!" And there was a correlative tendency to look askance at Brother Jo, who was always breaking silence: "Brother Jo is never going to make it in religious life—he can't walk by the news board without making some kind of loud comment!" More often than not, however, Brother Bo's easy way of keeping silence was linked more to his melancholic temperament than to virtue, and Brother Jo's easy faults in silence flowed from his sanguinity rather than from vice.

If we are honest, we have to admit that we tend to be selective in the external behaviors we praise. We are drawn to admire behaviors that we would like to cultivate more in our own lives, and so we tend to attribute them to moral capacities or spiritual maturity that we long to develop: "She never looks stressed or harried! She really has it all together. Those kids are so well-behaved—it's like they are the perfect family!" But this kind of attribution can distance us from the truth, distracting us from how God is working in our lives and leading us toward flattery, adulation, and the frustration that flows from setting up false ideals. It's a constant danger, because attributing perfection to a person we can see and touch seems to bring perfection down to our level. It appeals to the Pelagian tendency rooted in our cultural DNA ("Gosh, if I just try a little harder, I can make myself perfect, too, just like he did!"). Unfortunately, Pelagianism is a heresy. We cannot make ourselves perfect; we need the constant flow of God's grace to sanctify us.

The temptation to adulation can also contaminate how we live out one of Regnum Christi's core characteristics: love and veneration for the Holy Father. Every Catholic is obliged to show religious reverence for all the shepherds of the Church, and especially for the papacy. In Regnum Christi we take this obligation seriously. We truly believe that through the Vicar of Christ, the Lord himself "governs, teaches, and sanctifies us," as we pray in our traditional prayer for the Pope. We are especially sensitive to cultivating docility and loyalty to the Holy See because of the many Catholics and Catholic groups who consistently clash with Church authority and consider it a duty to dissent from even the most basic teachings found in the *Catechism*. We are defenders of Christ's Church, and that means we defend the Holy Father's teaching and follow his lead.

Dissent, however, isn't the only vice opposed to the virtue of reverence and obedience to Christ's Church and his Vicar on earth. Adulation (excessive obsequiousness) is another. Even holy popes make mistakes, and less holy popes make even more mistakes. The history of the Church shows clearly that this is the case. Our fidelity to the Holy Father is based on faith in Christ's promise that the papacy is the Church's rock-solid foundation: "You are Peter, and upon this rock I will build my church, and the gates of the netherworld shall not prevail against it" (Matthew 16:18). To base our reverence for a pope on anything else—his personality, his intellectual prowess, even his holiness—can actually weaken our faith. To treat every comment and decision the Holy Father makes as if it were on equal footing with Sacred Scripture can lead to an obfuscation of his authentic teaching. We must learn to receive what the popes give in the spirit in which they give it, allowing God's grace within us to let it nourish our souls.

All these warnings about flattery and adulation don't mean that we shouldn't admire and emulate good behavior when we see it. A friend who is faithful to his daily God-time regardless of the sacrifice involved, for example, can truly be a reminder and inspiration for us: "It is possible to make that happen; I want to make it happen in my life, too." It just means that being faithful to the truth in praising others requires a certain discipline. We need to avoid turning other people, even extremely accomplished and virtuous people, into idols. If we put others on a pedestal, we are bound to be disappointed. Only God is perfect; only the Lord is worthy of our worship. Even the saints had personality flaws and committed sins.

We also need to avoid exaggerated and only partially sincere encouragement and affirmation of other people. So often this morphs into a subtle form of flattery that gives us a feeling of being appreciated but gives no substantial help to the person we are trying to encourage or affirm. Adhering to the truth when giving words of encouragement and affirmation requires effort, discipline, and interior depth. We must know how to see beyond the surface and speak from a heart in tune with the depths of a true faith-perspective.

Looking for, acknowledging, and praising the good we see in others are habits that move us toward spiritual maturity, and we need to form them, even though we also need to discipline ourselves to avoid the exaggerations of flattery and adulation. The importance of learning to recognize the good in others follows logically from St. Paul's exhortation to the Philippians:

Finally, brothers, whatever is true, whatever is honorable, whatever is just, whatever is pure, whatever is lovely, whatever is gracious, if there is any excellence and if there is anything worthy of praise, think about these things.... Then the God of peace will be with you.

—Philippians 4:8–9

It is healthy to think good thoughts as long as they are true thoughts; it keeps us closer to God's wavelength. When we choose instead to dwell on the flaws and shortcomings of people and institutions, to pay exaggerated attention to them and talk about them unnecessarily, we spiral into a vortex of negativity that steals our own peace of mind and spreads like a poison to those around us.

DETRACTION

Detraction is often confused with calumny, but it involves an important distinction. Detraction holds to the truth; detraction is not lying. Yet it yields some of the same hideous by-products of calumny. According to the *Catechism*, someone falls into the temptation of detraction "who, without objectively valid reason, discloses another's faults and failings to persons who did not know them" (*CCC*, 2477). Calumny invents untrue faults and failings about people and spreads them around. Detraction takes people's true faults and failings and turns them into casual conversation topics.

We all have faults and failings; we publicly acknowledge this whenever we go to Mass: "I confess to almighty God, and to you my brothers and sisters, that I have greatly sinned, in my thoughts and in my words, in what I have done and in what I have failed to do, through my fault..." And yet who wants their faults and failings broadcast to all the earth? How does that help anyone?

Here again we see how easy it is to fall into hypocrisy—saying one thing and doing the opposite. We say it is unfair when someone spreads news about our own sins and flaws. And yet we so easily (and eagerly) like to share with others any news we hear about the sins and flaws of others. This kind of gossip, as in the case of rash judgment, appeals to our desire to feel superior. When we spread dirt about other people, even if it's real dirt, we somehow feel that we are above the mess, conveniently forgetting about the many times that we too have fallen into the dirt of disgraceful and shameful behavior. A good rule of thumb to help curb this tendency is to refrain from saying anything about someone who is not present that we wouldn't say if that person were present.

Detraction applies to the people we interact with on a regular basis— friends, colleagues, family members. But it also applies to people we may never meet—politicians, celebrities, anyone who finds themselves in the public spotlight. Somehow our popular culture has concluded that those people have no right to privacy. Their personal lives are treated as fodder for mass entertainment. We all have a tendency to enjoy sharing inside stories about the foibles of famous people. And yet, even when the foibles are true, we need to ask ourselves what good this type of communication produces. It certainly produces nothing good for the people whose private lives are constantly being exposed to public scrutiny; it only makes their lives more burdensome. Is that a fair exchange?

Detraction involves disclosing peoples' faults to those who do not know them *without an objectively valid reason*. This implies that sometimes we will have good reason to disclose people's faults and failings. When those faults could cause damage to another person, we may be justified in revealing them to relevant individuals or groups. This applies to cases of criminal activity, for example. But it could also apply in a more mundane situation, as when an executive is helping an outside consultant to prepare for an off-site meeting; it would be useful for the consultant to know the strengths and weaknesses of the executive's team members. Or when someone's failings are beginning to destroy that person himself, we may feel obliged to reveal them to third parties (family members, friends, clergy) in order to try and get necessary help. In those cases, however, we should always try to go the person in question first, when we perceive a reasonable chance for that person to make a change. This is a healthy form of fraternal correction, a truly evangelical value:

If your brother sins [against you], go and tell him his fault between you and him alone. If he listens to you, you have won over your brother. If he does not listen, take one or two others along with you, so that 'every fact may be established on the testimony of two or three witnesses.' If he refuses to listen to them, tell the church. If he refuses to listen even to the church, then treat him as you would a Gentile or a tax collector.

—Matthew 18:15–17

A proper understanding of *benediciencia* flows from a clear appreciation of the damage calumny and detraction do to individuals and communities. Habitually discussing other peoples' faults and failings, whether real, imagined, or invented, creates a climate of suspicion and mistrust. Relationships, projects, and communities wither in that arid climate. Habitually focusing on the strengths and possibilities of people and situations creates a climate of hope, mutual appreciation, and productivity. In that climate, relationships, projects, and communities have a much better chance to flourish. This doesn't require ignoring obvious faults and failings. Rather, it means that we prefer to see those realities for what they truly are—only part of the story, and the less important part at that.

DEGRADING IRONY, BOASTING, AND DESTRUCTIVE CRITICISM

Like detraction, degrading irony and destructive criticism adhere to the truth, but they still qualify as abusive uses of communication. Unlike detraction, however, these forms of speech directly address the person being cut down. Insults like these sometimes erupt during angry arguments, like verbal blows meant to punish, humiliate, or intimidate someone we feel has wronged us. At other times we wield them with calculated purpose in order to manipulate others and get what we want. In certain contexts and relationships, these forms of verbal abuse become barely perceptible habits, ingrained patterns of behavior that need to be rooted out through repentance and the renewing power of grace.

Good-humored irony brings enjoyment, laughter, and stimulation to conversation. When it wounds other people, however, it crosses the line from spice to poison. Sincere concern for others requires us to pay attention to the effect our comments have on those around us. What one person may take in stride and enjoy may feel like a slap in the face or a personal attack to someone else. When laughter is bought at the expense of someone's tears, the price is simply too high.

The *Catechism* warns against boasting or bragging in the same paragraph it warns against degrading irony. A boast may include a dose of the truth, but more often than not, it also includes an exaggeration. Even more than obscuring the truth, however, boasting mimics degrading irony in its attempt to belittle other people. When we brag, we are attempting to elevate ourselves over others; the tone and often the content of a boast show a certain disdain for people who have achieved less than we have. Instead of drawing people together and encouraging them, this kind of speech demeans and discourages.

Constructive criticism, like good-humored irony, is a necessary ingredient in human interaction. When fear of other people's reactions habitually impedes us from sharing our relevant insights and wisdom, something is wrong. As human beings we need each other. No single person has all the answers. No individual can solve every problem alone. Being created in the image of God means, among other things, that we are called to lean on each other as we make our way through the adventure of life: God is a Trinity of Persons—a family, a team—and we are created to image that interpersonal communion in everything we do. This means that each person's gifts, talents, and skills are real but incomplete. We need the gifts, talents, and skills of others in order for ours to flourish. St. Paul explains this reality by comparing the Church, the body of Christ, to a human body:

But as it is, God placed the parts, each one of them, in the body as he intended. If they were all one part, where would the body be? But as it is, there are many parts, yet one body. The eye cannot say to the hand, "I do not need you," nor again the head to the feet, "I do not need you."

—I Corinthians 12:18–21

This intrinsic need we each have for others underlies the distinction between constructive and destructive criticism. Constructive criticism points out how something can be improved, and it does so in a way that invites the person being criticized to see, appreciate, and desire that potential improvement. Destructive criticism doesn't.

When criticism—insights into potential improvements—consists solely of complaints about things over which we have no influence, it weighs us (and everybody who is forced to listen to us) down, instead of building us up. Cynical critics always have at the ready a witty quip about why this won't work or that will never get off the ground. But they stop there, revealing a dangerous streak of passivity. It's as if they are not really interested in seeing progress, success, or improvement. Somehow the critic almost seems pleased with stagnation or failure. This can be an outgrowth of pride, envy, and other forms of personal insecurity.

CONSTRUCTIVE CRITICISM

On the other hand, legitimate criticism can be given in a manner, a time, or a circumstance that makes it almost impossible for the person being criticized to receive it positively. It may be intended as constructive criticism, but it is received as destructive criticism. Truly concerned and constructive critics make an effort to discern the proper context for making their contributions. Sometimes we need to wait until strong emotions have calmed down. Other times we need to invest in a relationship through affirmation and cooperation until it is strong enough to benefit from healthy criticism.

Constructive criticism requires vulnerability, both on the part of the critic and the part of the criticized. Since we all have our own wounds and weaknesses, such vulnerability can be challenging. One tactic that helps create safe environments for this crucial kind of communication is the establishment of forums for feedback.

When a team of people working on the same apostolate, for example, devotes a specific time each week or month to give each other constructive criticism, holding each accountable to the commitments they have made, it's easier to take. Going into the meeting, the members are already expecting to be mutually vulnerable, and so they are ready and willing to give and accept constructive criticism.

Likewise in a marriage, if a couple creates space every week—a real meeting time, for example—to go over their goals and behaviors together, asking for and being open to receiving constructive criticism, the tension that can naturally build up around difficult issues has a natural release point. Fruitless nagging, moody complaining, and silent indignation have fewer opportunities to dig in their destructive claws and wound the trust and mutual acceptance so necessary for ongoing growth in intimacy and friendship among spouses.

Creating a forum for feedback, a habitual space in which constructive criticism can be given and received, is essential for any human group to be able to reach its full potential. Much of the literature surrounding good business management, for instance, wrestles with effective ways to create forums where healthy vulnerability allows for healthy criticism to create its unique and necessary synergy. In sports and in the arts, much of the rhythm of training flows from specific time given to coaches and directors for analyzing film of previous games or performances together with the players and performers.

Even in those forums, however, merely saying what's wrong is not enough. The manner in which critical insights are given is equally as important as the content of those insights. I know one extremely successful theatre director, for example, who never gives more than three observations to any individual actor after any one rehearsal. She knows from experience that even if she has more than three observations to give, few actors have enough bandwidth to accept and digest four or more.

One reason constructive criticism requires mutual vulnerability is because it often leads to conflict. If a teenager makes a bad decision and his dad calls him on it, the son will naturally want to defend himself. We always make our decisions for a reason, and even when the reason was wrong, we can feel compelled to explain it. That means conflict. Dad says X; son says Y. Is this bad? Is conflict intrinsically evil, contrary to charity? No. Often only the exchange of conflicting points of view can result in real growth and deeper understanding. Many times new insights and solutions can only emerge through the passionate juxtaposition of opposing opinions. Discussion breeds clarity.

Conflict—the exchange of differing perspectives—can become unhealthy and destructive depending on how it is handled. If differences over ideas and procedures start overflowing into personal attacks, the discussion can degenerate quickly. If the discomfort caused by voicing different opinions triggers self-defense mechanisms and leads to someone withdrawing from the exchange out of irrational fear, it has the power to transform potentially fruitful conflict into an exercise in resentment and frustration. For conflict to stay healthy, it must stay focused on the problem at hand, and all parties need to be sure that each one really is seeking the truth and vying for what is better for everyone involved.

VENTING VERSUS WHINING

Sometimes we just need to vent—to voice out loud all the things that are frustrating us about a particular relationship or situation, regardless of whether or not our frustrations are justified. In a venting session, we are not interesting in being constructive; we just need to let off some steam, and that involves addressing the faults and failings of other people. It can be pure complaining, without offering any solutions at all. Is this ever healthy? Is venting ever okay?

Of course it is. We have to process strong emotions. We have to integrate them into our consciousness and our relationship with God. Part of the process involves *naming* those emotions. Healthy venting focuses on expressing in words, to a mature and trustworthy person with a wise and sympathetic ear, the strong emotions we feel.

Venting can become destructive, however, and even sinful, when we allow ourselves to switch focus. When venting becomes more about what's wrong with everyone else rather than the emotional waves that are crashing onto the shore of our own soul, it becomes destructive. Certainly other people's faults and failings can be triggers for some of our own emotional waves. It is no sin to admit that. But ultimately we are responsible for how we react to those waves and those triggers. We are rarely pure victims. We can choose to forgive, to focus on what is within our control, to step away from negative influences. Venting helps us process our own emotions, but it is never a legitimate excuse for judging, blaming, and otherwise verbally shredding other people.

Venting can also become unhealthy when we choose to vent to the wrong person. When we need to let off steam, we have to be prudent about where we send it. The Bible often shows prayer as a safe arena for venting—peruse the Book of Psalms or the Book of Job, for example. God knows how to hear our complaints, sorrows, and frustrations. Often a psalm that begins with an impassioned complaint transitions into a peaceful and refreshed expression of trust and confidence in God; Psalm 13 is one example.

Spiritual direction is another safe place for venting. A trustworthy spiritual director will be careful to avoid drawing conclusions about other people from what is said in venting mode. The spiritual director can also help us process the emotions we need to process by bathing them in the light of faith and common sense. A good friend, a mentor, a parent—when we need to vent, we should choose someone who knows us well and won't be drawn into the tangled situations that may have produced the intense emotions we are feeling, someone mature, who knows how to listen well and won't overreact. Immature or self-interested listeners may give us a sense of being affirmed, but they may also be scandalized by what we tell them, or feel obliged to intervene, forgetting that venting isn't about solving problems, but processing emotions. We each should have one or two (not twelve or thirteen) people to whom we can vent when necessary. If we find ourselves venting to anyone and everyone, something is wrong; healthy venting has morphed into witless whining.

"THIS NEED NOT BE SO"

Some manuals of moral theology would dig deeper into the subtler distinctions of all these sins. Yet, as mentioned above, even though casuistry has its place, it can too easily become a tangle and a distraction. Whenever we find ourselves passionately quibbling, it's best to take a step back and try to see the forest for the trees, to make sure we are truly spending our time and energy wisely. As St. Paul warned St. Timothy: "Avoid foolish and ignorant debates, for you know that they breed quarrels" (2 Timothy 2:23).

Many positive ways to use words came up when we looked at common sins related to the eighth commandment. The power of words for good, however, extends far beyond the foundational virtue of truthfulness. Avoiding lies, detraction, and flattery is the essential prerequisite for growing in this sector of our spiritual life. Yet this arena of virtue expands far beyond merely avoiding faults. Any mature Christian should sincerely value words, their beauty, and their power. And we in the Regnum Christi Movement have made doing so an explicit value in our spirituality. We have singled it out.

Regnum Christi members should be known for their firm and almost automatic refusal to waste time in useless, destructive criticism and relationship-poisoning gossip sessions. But we also make a commitment to use our capacity of speech for good, to develop the art of communication so that we can truly minister to others with our words. Charity in speech requires that, at least as we have always understood it in our spiritual family.

What remains of this Essay, then, will explore a few essential elements in developing that art, in sharpening our tongue for good.

INTANGIBLES

When some people talk, we really want to listen. It's not necessarily because they are exceptionally intelligent, witty, or creative. Rather, it's something about what lies behind their actual words. They may say something we have heard a hundred times ("God is faithful; everything will work out okay"), but when *they* say it, it strikes a chord deep in our hearts; it makes us pause. What's the special sauce that gives these people's words so much weight?

Classical communication theory might call it conviction. Whenever people are deeply, thoughtfully, and thoroughly convinced about something, this conviction gives their discourse a certain mysterious power. Beyond mere rhetorical technique, speaking from the heart gives our words authenticity. They ring true. Since they come from our heart, they have a better chance of reaching our listeners' heart: cor ad cor loquitur ("heart speaks to heart"), as St. Francis de Sales put it (a phrase Blessed John Henry Newman chose as his motto when he was named Cardinal in 1879). That's just the way it is. That's how we were made to communicate. Not superficially, not with a lot of fancy phrases that give the impression of wisdom and make a superficial splash, but with real wisdom that resonates in the deeper levels of the human soul. This is how Jesus spoke:

Never before has anyone spoken like this one...

—John 7:46

When Jesus finished these words, the crowds were astonished at his teaching, for he taught them as one having authority, and not as their scribes.

—Matthew 7:28—29

Even in secular contexts, leadership and communication experts emphasize the importance of speaking from deep conviction, not just saying what we think we are expected to say. Otherwise real communication simply doesn't happen; conversations are merely smokescreens and self-defensive posturing rather than true and transforming human encounters.

Speaking from the heart, from our deepest convictions, often requires a willingness to be vulnerable. But it also requires *having* deep convictions. This is where one's interior life becomes an essential ingredient in effective communication. A sharp arrow will penetrate its target more deeply if it is shot from a stronger bow. The hidden power of our words is connected to how deeply we ourselves have been penetrated by the Word. We can better speak life to others the more we ourselves are filled with the abundant and gracified life of our Lord.

SILENCE

In order to hear, there must be silence. Think about it: If you are in the midst of a cacophony—maybe in the middle of a raucous crowd gyrating manically in the heat of a wild rock concert—you can't hear the specific words someone speaks to you personally. They are drowned out by the intense noise. There is just no room for them to resonate; they are violently washed away by the tsunami of sound.

Silence is the space in which words communicate their message. Like the empty space inside the chamber of a violin, or in the hollow part of a canoe, silence allows the words to resonate, to travel, to be heard. To become excellent communicators, then, we must learn to appreciate silence and give it a place in our lives.

In the digital age, this poses particular challenges. Words and images—audible and visual noise—tend to engulf us at every turn. Today we must be more intentional about creating space for silence and deep listening than in any period of human history that has come before us. Certainly only a few of us are called to a religious or monastic lifestyle built precisely to maximize the power of silence in pursuit of a deep interior life, but all of us are meant to value the importance of silence. Time spent in adoration of the Blessed Sacrament, in contemplating the beauty of great art and nature, in driving at times without the accompaniment of phone calls and podcasts, in doing chores sometimes without having our earbuds plugged in—these are just several of the many ways we can maintain space in our souls where words, and the Word, can always find a proper welcome.

Silence also has a part to play, not only in creating a receptive interior atmosphere, but in disciplining our own speech. Often we feel moved to speak when we should refrain from speaking. Often our words flow not from a pure intention of contributing and building communion, but from fears and a desperate need to seek attention or to justify an action that may have been misinterpreted. Often we blurt things out imprudently, instead of listening and reflecting calmly before speaking. Without humility and discipline in this regard, we can create a lot of unnecessary problems.

This is another favorite theme in the Book of Proverbs:

> When there are many words, transgression is unavoidable, but he who restrains his lips is wise.
>
> ——Proverbs 10:19

> He who restrains his words has knowledge, and he who has a cool spirit is a man of understanding. Even a fool, when he keeps silent, is considered wise; when he closes his lips, he is considered prudent.
>
> ——Proverbs 17:27–28

St. James picks up on this theme as well: "This you know, my beloved brethren. But everyone must be quick to hear, slow to speak and slow to anger" (James 1:19).

Excessive talking, or saying the wrong thing at the wrong time, leads to unedifying speech. Often it is a symptom of some other interior dysfunction that needs to be exposed to God's grace for healing. In this context words can be shields defending unhealthy fears and desperate, subconscious pleas for affection or validation. Here we have a fruitful area for self-reflection and discussion in spiritual direction.

Finally, we should mention the art of listening and the art of conversation. These really are arts. At first glance they don't appear to be, because we all learn to do both without even thinking about them. Listening and conversing are capacities built into our human nature. Even two-year-olds listen and converse.

And yet we have all had the experience of truly being listened to by someone who has developed the basic capacity of hearing into a true art. When we finally find someone who really hears what we say and what we mean, it's like finding an oasis in the desert. A real *connection* happens; a real *communication*, an establishment of communion, takes place. With others, as much as we try to express ourselves, we sense that nothing is really penetrating whatever filters our listener—whether culpably or not—has activated. Few experiences can be as frustrating, or even disheartening.

This phenomenon shows that the ability to listen well can be developed. It also shows that good listening is a rich expression of charity and authentic concern for another person. One of our deepest needs as human beings is to be known and understood. Someone who has learned the art of listening has learned to slake that deep, existential thirst.

Counselors, psychologists, social workers, and many other professionals study the art of listening intentionally and formally. This shows that growth and improvement in this natural human capacity is possible, and that many smart people have developed ways to foster that growth. Because of our commitment to spread Christ's kingdom by loving others truly and substantially, we should make an effort to benefit from all that practical wisdom.

Conversation too can be more or less edifying, effective, and enjoyable. We all know people we enjoy talking with.

Whatever the topic, whatever the context, we just like having them at the table, so to speak. They always seem to help make the flow of conversation better somehow. Everyone is more involved and seems to get more out of it when this person is part of the exchange. And when the good conversationalist is absent, everyone feels it. The atmosphere gets heavy. Awkward silences multiply. People start looking at their watches more quickly, and stimulating connections just don't seem to happen in quite the same way.

Is this just because some people are naturally better at this than others? To a certain extent, yes. Some people tend to be the life of the party just because of their personality. And yet even those personalities become tiresome unless they learn to be conversational team players. The life-of-the-party personality can be entertaining, especially for new acquaintances and in small portions. But without the seasoning provided by having developed the art of conversation, they can quickly become overbearing, if not obnoxious.

Personalities can be more or less sociable, and we can't do much about which end of the spectrum our temperament and early upbringing has put us on. But we can all develop and improve our ability to contribute to engaging, edifying, and enjoyable conversation, precisely because it is an art.

In past ages the art of conversation was recognized and taught explicitly. A Renaissance man, for example, was required to learn how to speak intelligently on any topic that might come up in conversation. He was also instructed and practiced in the forms of etiquette so that he could help others (and himself) overcome nervousness or shyness within different social settings. He was exposed to a wide variety of cultural experiences so as to deepen his sensitivity to and appreciation for the rich variety of human personalities and modes of expression.

Certainly, the art of conversation as it developed in aristocratic Europe often degenerated into a mere formalism, an empty shell of civility that disguised duplicity and angst. But the abuse of something doesn't take away its use.

One of the most traditional and heartwarming forms of charity, in the long tradition of Christianity, is hospitality. We all recognize that a truly and sincerely gracious host will find ways to make guests feel at home, to help them relax and enter into the healthy circle of interaction present in any family or community. The art of conversation is a subset of that—it is hospitality in speech, so to speak. It is a form of loving others by finding gentle and respectful ways to involve them in the exchange of thoughts and ideas that conversation entails. Some simple rules of politeness—such as paying attention when someone else is speaking, not interrupting, and not always speaking about oneself—go far in producing good conversation. But the true art can develop only when we begin to see all conversation, like listening, as an opportunity to love and be loved, to build up Christ's kingdom through engaging, edifying, and enjoyable verbal interaction. When that attitude translates into a practical desire to develop this capacity, the rest will follow.

CONCLUSION

Words matter. The Bible tells us that they do, as does common sense, experience, and philosophy. Words are unique to human beings, and so they are connected to every dimension of what makes us who we are. When St. James asserts, "If anyone does not fall short in speech, he is a perfect man," he isn't exaggerating (James 3:2). Maturity in this arena of virtue, as in every arena of virtue, involves habitually avoiding the evil abuses of speech, such as calumny and detraction. It also involves developing a deeper appreciation for truth and the words that express truth, and learning to use words in ways that build up all that is good in the human endeavor and purify all that is bad.

We use thousands of words every day. Imagine how much good we could do if we gradually developed our capacity to infuse more and more of those words with truly Christlike wisdom and love. As Regnum Christi members, Catholic Christians eager not only to defend the borders of Christ's kingdom but also extend them, may we always seek to do so.

APPENDICES

APPENDIX I: A PRACTICAL EXAMINATION OF CONSCIENCE ON CHARITY IN WORDS

1. How would I describe my general attitude toward words? Respectful, indifferent, awe-filled…?

2. How would I describe in my own words the role language and communication are meant to play in human life?

3. When have I been hurt or wounded by words? As I reflect on those experiences, I will compare them to the hurt that Christ and Mary experienced because of malicious words. How fully have I forgiven those who may have hurt me?

4. When have I felt encouraged and affirmed by words? I will take some time to reflect on that experience, enjoy it, and thank God for it.

5. What words in Sacred Scripture have nourished me consistently through the years? I will list the most relevant passages, savor them, and find a way to keep them close throughout the busy-ness of life.

6. How would I explain in my own words what these sins consist of: lying, calumny (slander), detraction, flattery, adulation, destructive criticism, degrading irony, and rash judgment?

7. Which of those sins do I find most tempting in my day-to-day interactions? Why?

8. How would I describe in my own words the difference between flattery and encouragement?

9. How would I describe in my own words the difference between flattery and healthy affirmation?

10. How would I describe in my own words the difference between proper respect and exaggerated adulation?

11. What circumstances tend to lead me to say things I regret? Why? How can I ready myself to resist those temptations better? How can I avoid those circumstances altogether?

12. How much do I value silence in my life?

13. What personal habits unnecessarily create extra noise (audible, visual, or otherwise) in my daily life? How can I change those habits?

14. When have I really felt listened to and understood? What made me feel that way?

15. On a scale of one to ten, how would I rate myself as a listener? In which relationships or roles of my life do I most need to become a better listener? What can I do this week to start making that happen?

16. Who are the best conversationalists I know? What makes them so good at the art of conversation?

17. On a scale of one to ten, how would I rate myself as a conversationalist? In what circumstances do I tend to be a good conversationalist, and in what circumstances do I tend to be a poor one? Why?

18. What can I do this week to refine the art of conversation in my life?

APPENDIX 2: A GUIDE FOR GROUP DISCUSSION ON SHARPENING YOUR TONGUE

[A Note for Facilitators: Each member of your group should read the Essay ahead of time with these questions in mind, and come prepared to share their answers. Take as many sessions as necessary to discuss fully. You may want to come up with additional questions for discussion based on your group's own experiences, ideas, and needs.]

1. What if anything did I learn in this RC Essay that I didn't know before?

2. What three insights offered by this RC Essay made the biggest impression on me and why?

3. What is the most positive and negative life experience I have had in relation to the topic of this essay?

4. What insight offered by this RC Essay is most valuable for helping me to improve my family life?

5. What insight offered by this RC Essay is most valuable for helping me to improve my prayer life?

6. What insight offered by this RC Essay is most valuable for helping my social and/or professional life?

7. Who are some public figures that generally model good use of speech? How does their good example affect their ability to communicate and to find listeners?

8. How would a non-Catholic react to the content of this RC Essay? How could I respond constructively to that reaction?

9. How would a non-Christian react to the content of this RC Essay? How could I respond constructively to that reaction?

10. How can we as a group help each other assimilate and grow as a result of what we read in this RC Essay? How can we help keep each other accountable?

11. Where does our popular culture stand in relation to the values discussed in this RC Essay? How does that culture affect us positively and negatively? How can we positively affect that culture?

EXPLORING MORE

Please visit our website, *RCSpirituality.org* for more spiritual resources, and follow us on Facebook for regular updates: *facebook.com/RCSpirituality*

Regnum Christi Essays are a service of Regnum Christi and the Legionaries of Christ. *RegnumChristi.org* & *LegionofChrist.org*

Produced by Coronation. *CoronationMedia.com*

Developed & Self-published by RCSpirituality. *RCSpirituality.org*